THE Presidents OF THE UNITED STATES

Before he enters on the Execution of his Office, he shall take the following Oath or Affirmation—

"I do solemnly swear that I will faithfully execute the Office of President of the United States, and will to the best of my Ability, preserve, protect and defend the Constitution of the United States."

from The U.S. Constitution, Article II, Section I

THE Presidents OF THE UNITED STATES

ROBIN LANGLEY SOMMER

BARNES & NOBLE
BOOKS
NEW YORK

FOR

EUGENE CARR

Beloved Irish carpenter

Cover photograph: George Washington, *by Gilbert Stuart*
Reproduced by permission of The Granger Collection

Produced by DoveTail Books

Produced in association with Saraband Inc.

This edition published by Barnes & Noble, Inc.
by arrangement with DoveTail Books

1997 Barnes & Noble Books

ISBN 0-7607-0319-1

Printed in China

1 3 5 7 9 8 6 4 2

Foreword

In an article from *The Federalist* (1787–88), a series of essays written in defense of the proposed Constitution, Alexander Hamilton wrote of the vital importance of a strong, independent chief executive: "Energy in the executive is a leading character in the definition of good government. It is essential to the protection of the community against foreign attacks; it is not less essential to the steady administration of the laws, to the protection of property...[and] to the security of liberty against the enterprises and assaults of ambition, of faction, and of anarchy."

More than forty men have filled the office of president of the United States since George Washington's first inauguration on April 30, 1789. Some of them, like Washington, Thomas Jefferson, and James Madison, were remarkable statesmen and legislators before they achieved the presidency. Others grew to their full stature through the exigencies of their office, as did Abraham Lincoln in the crucible of civil war and Franklin D. Roosevelt through the Great Depression and World War II. Still others, like Theodore Roosevelt and Harry S. Truman, were thrust into the presidency by the death of the incumbent, whether by violence or natural causes, and distinguished themselves beyond expectations—including, perhaps, their own. Of course, not everyone who has served as president was equal to the role. Some were politically naive, like Ulysses S. Grant, who relied too much on untrustworthy advisors. Richard M. Nixon, with good abilities, resigned under the cloud of illegal political machinations. Some men found the vast responsibility and publicity too much for them and left the White House with profound relief to return to private life.

Others were simply decent, humane, hard-working people who gave of their best. However, all of their stories are of deep historical and human interest. They are presented here in brief as an informative overview of those who have filled the nation's highest office.

Contents

George Washington

1732–99
1ST PRESIDENT
Federalist
Term: 1789–97

Vice-President: John Adams
First Lady:
Martha Dandridge Custis

Born in Westmoreland County, Virginia, to an old colonial family, the nation's first president had only seven or eight years of formal education before he became a surveyor at the age of sixteen. In 1749 he helped lay out the new town of Alexandria, Virginia, and was appointed official surveyor for Culpeper County. At the same time, he helped manage his family plantation, Ferry Farm, and invested his earnings in more land. In 1752 he inherited the extensive property known as Mount Vernon through his half-brother, Lawrence Washington. He spent much of his life improving his holdings there and building the house overlooking the Potomac River that would become a national shrine.

Washington's military career began in 1753, and he was to distinguish himself through his service as a militia major (later colonel) in the French and Indian War of 1755–63. He led the troops that defended Virginia's 350-mile frontier and served with British general Edward Braddock in the attempt to capture Fort Duquesne (present-day Pittsburgh) in 1755. Braddock was fatally wounded, and Washington had two horses shot from under him before the engagement ended in defeat. After the war, he married the widow Martha Dandridge Custis and became a devoted stepfather to her son and daughter, John Parke and Martha Parke Custis.

From 1759 Washington was a member of the Virginia House of Burgesses. On the eve of the American Revolution, the Second Continental Congress elected him commander-in-chief of the Continental Army, which he led through great difficulties from 1775 until his victory over British general Charles Cornwallis at Yorktown, Virginia, in October 1781. He seldom had more than 10,000 troops at any given time, and his makeshift army was plagued by desertion, poor training, short enlistments, and scarce supplies, especially during the grueling winter of 1777–8 at Valley Forge, Pennsylvania. Washington won national renown as a courageous and patriotic leader for his heroic role in the war. He headed the convention that wrote the U.S. Constitution in 1787 and was elected the new nation's first president.

Inaugurated in New York City in 1789, Washington served as president for two terms, declining a third in his famous "Farewell Address." Determined to create a free and democratic nation fulfilling the principles of the Constitution, he had remained above party conflict and regional alliances throughout his presidency and effectively established the new system of government: the Chief Executive, Congress, and Supreme Court, providing leadership with separation of power. He had presided over the growth of the union from eleven to fifteen states; passage of the Bill of Rights (1791); establishment of the Department of Foreign Affairs (now the Department of State); suppression of the Whiskey Rebellion of 1794, the first armed opposition to the federal government; and establishment of the national capital at Washington, D.C.

Washington spent his last few years at Mount Vernon, relieved of the burden of public office, which he had assumed "with diffidence and reluctance." His friend and secretary of state Thomas Jefferson eulogized him with the words: "Perhaps the strongest feature in his character was prudence, never acting until every circumstance, every consideration, was maturely weighed; refraining when he saw a doubt, but when once decided, going through with his purpose whatever obstacles opposed. His integrity was most pure, his justice the most inflexible that I have ever known."

"Labor to keep alive in your breast that little spark of celestial fire called conscience."

— George Washington

John Adams

1735–1826
2ND PRESIDENT
Federalist
Term: 1797–1801
Vice-President:
Thomas Jefferson
First Lady: Abigail Smith

John Adams, a native of Massachusetts, came from a family that had settled in Boston during the 1630s. He graduated from Harvard College in 1755 and married Abigail Smith, with whom he had five children. Their long and affectionate correspondence during his public life would become a valuable contribution to American history and letters.

With Thomas Jefferson, Adams worked on the Declaration of Independence in 1776 and helped to negotiate the Treaty of Paris with Great Britain (1783) after the Revolutionary War. He served as Washington's vice-president from 1789 and was elected president in 1796—the first chief executive to live in the White House, which was still unfinished when he took up residence there. A moderate Federalist, Adams was constantly at odds with his Cabinet. His major contribution was the establishment of a strong American navy and the maintenance of American neutrality in the face of the Anglo-French hostilities that followed the French Revolution.

Adams lost the presidential election of 1800 but lived to see his son, John Quincy Adams, elected the sixth president. Both Thomas Jefferson and John Adams died on July 4, 1826, the fiftieth anniversary of the Declaration of Independence.

Thomas Jefferson

1743–1826
3RD PRESIDENT
Democratic-Republican
Term: 1801–1809

Vice-Presidents:
Aaron Burr, 1801–05
George Clinton, 1805–09
First Lady: None
(widowed in 1782)

Thomas Jefferson, one of the most distinguished statesmen in history, was born in Albemarle County, Virginia, at Shadwell, a 2,500-acre estate. He attended the College of William & Mary, studied law, and became a member of the Virginia House of Burgesses, where he began a sixty-year career in public service.

In 1770 Jefferson began designing his famous country house, Monticello, and two years later he married Martha Wayles Skelton. Of their six children, only two daughters lived to maturity. Jefferson never remarried after his wife's death in 1782.

Jefferson's most memorable single work is the Declaration of Independence, which set forth the philosophy of constitutional government and the case for the American Revolution (1776). He produced it at the Second Continental Congress, after which he served as governor of Virginia (1779–81) and American envoy to France (1784). In 1789 he accepted George Washington's offer of the Cabinet post as minister for foreign affairs. His democratic sympathy for the French Revolutionaries, and economic issues, brought him into conflict with Alexander Hamilton, secretary of the treasury.

In 1797 Jefferson became John Adams's vice-president. He was elected president in 1801 by the Democratic-Republican Party, which opposed Adams's Federalist policies. Jefferson's two terms of office saw the purchase of the vast Louisiana Territory; passage by Congress of a law banning the slave trade; the Lewis and Clark expedition; and the Embargo Act of 1807.

Jefferson left the White House in 1809 and spent the rest of his life pursuing other diverse interests, including architecture, agriculture, music, writing, and education. In 1819 he designed and founded the University of Virginia at Charlottesville. The 50th anniversary of the Declaration of Independence was marked by the death of Jefferson.

James Madison

1751–1836
4TH PRESIDENT
Democratic-Republican
Term: 1809–17
Vice-Presidents: George Clinton,
1809–Apr. 20, 1812
Elbridge Gerry,
1813–Nov. 23, 1814
First Lady: Dolley Payne Todd

A native of Port Conway, Virginia, Madison attended what is now Princeton University and entered public life as a member of the Virginia Constitutional Committee of 1776. His Virginia Plan would form the basis for many sections of the federal Constitution. In 1779 Madison was elected to the Continental Congress, and in 1787 he became a principal architect of the U.S. Constitution. He was the author of many of the Federalist papers urging its ratification.

In 1794 Madison married the widowed Dolley Payne Todd, who would become one of the nation's most popular and vivacious first ladies. Elected to the first House of Representatives as a Federalist, Madison served throughout Washington's administration, moving gradually toward a Democratic-Republican stance. He was prominent in securing adoption of the Bill of Rights.

In 1801 Madison entered Jefferson's cabinet as secretary of state, and in 1808 he was elected president. His popular support eroded during the War of 1812 with Great Britain, but he was re-elected to a second term, after which he retired to Montpelier, his Virginia estate.

James Monroe

1758–1831
5TH PRESIDENT
Term: 1817–25
Democratic-Republican
Vice-President:
Daniel D. Tompkins
First Lady:
Elizabeth Kortright

Like so many of the Founding Fathers, Monroe was born in Virginia (Westmoreland County). He attended the College of William & Mary before enlisting for service in the Revolutionary War, where he served with distinction. He then studied law and held several offices in Virginia state politics. In 1794 he went to France as U.S. minister and in 1803 helped to negotiate the Louisiana Purchase.

Opposed to Federalist policies, Monroe became active in the Democratic-Republican Party. He was appointed secretary of state during Madison's administration and served as secretary of war for a short time. In 1816 he was elected president. With the help of his secretary of state John Quincy Adams, he formulated the Monroe Doctrine (1823), which warned that the United States would not tolerate European interference in the affairs of the Western Hemisphere. During Monroe's administration, the nation grew from fifteen to twenty-four states. His presidency was called the "Era of Good Feelings" because there were no severe external threats to the country and party politics were less acrimonious than they had been for some years. At the end of his second term, Monroe retired to private life.

John Quincy Adams

1767–1848
6TH PRESIDENT
Democratic-Republican
Term: 1825–29
Vice-President:
John C. Calhoun
First Lady:
Louisa Catherine Johnson

The sixth president was the only one to hold the office after his own father had. Born near Boston, in Quincy, Massachusetts, the eldest son of statesman John Adams, he traveled with his father on diplomatic missions from the age of eleven and was educated mainly abroad. After graduating from Harvard in 1787, Adams served in various diplomatic posts and as a senator from Massachusetts (elected 1803). He was minister to the Netherlands, Britain, and Prussia before serving as secretary of state to Monroe (1817–25), whom he helped to formulate the Monroe Doctrine of 1823.

In 1824 Adams, a nominal Federalist, ran for president against three Southerners: Henry Clay, Andrew Jackson, and William H. Crawford. The hotly debated election resulted in a narrow victory for Adams, with Clay's support, but his other two opponents balked at most of the legislation he proposed to Congress, claiming he had made a "corrupt bargain" with Clay. Adams wrote of his years in the White House that "I can scarcely conceive a more harassing, wearying, teasing condition of existence." After losing the election of 1828 to Jackson, Adams was elected to the House of Representatives, where he served happily for seventeen years.

Andrew Jackson

1767–1845
7TH PRESIDENT
Democrat
Term: 1829–37
Vice-Presidents:
John C. Calhoun, 1829–32
Martin Van Buren, 1833–37
First Lady: None
(widowed 1828)

The first populist president, Jackson was born in Waxhaw, South Carolina, to a frontier family. He studied law and became public prosecutor of what is now Tennessee. In 1891 he married Rachel Donelson Robards, a divorcée.

During the War of 1812, Jackson led the Tennessee militia to victories over the Creek Indians (1813) and a large British force at the Battle of New Orleans (1815). He was elected to the U.S. Senate as a hero in 1823, although many Washington aristocrats took a dim view of this rough-hewn country soldier, whose temper was legendary. Jackson lost the presidential election of 1824 to John Quincy Adams, but proceeded to defeat him in 1828. Shortly after his victory, Jackson's wife died of a heart attack. He blamed his political opponents, who had used her divorced status against him during the campaign.

As president, Jackson introduced the "spoils system" of political patronage and relied for advice on a few close friends who became popularly known as the "Kitchen Cabinet." He ruthlessly pursued the policy of Indian removal to lands west of the Mississippi and undermined the Bank of the United States. His years in office saw the establishment of the nation's first political machine on the federal level.

Martin Van Buren

1782–1862
8TH PRESIDENT
Democrat
Term: 1837–41
Vice-President:
Richard M. Johnson
First Lady: None
(widowed 1819)

A descendant of Dutch immigrants, Van Buren, from Kinderhook, New York, studied law and was admitted to the bar in 1803. In 1807 he married his cousin Hannah Hoes, who died in 1819. He became a New York state senator (1812) and state attorney general (1816). Elected to the U.S. Senate as a Democratic-Republican in 1821, he resigned to become governor of New York in 1828.

Van Buren was instrumental in securing the election of President Andrew Jackson, who made him secretary of state in 1829. Three years later he was elected Jackson's vice-president. A sophisticated politician, Van Buren seemed an unlikely partner for the soldier-frontiersman, but the two worked well together. In 1836 Van Buren was elected president with Jackson's support, but the severe depression that began with the Panic of 1837 cast a cloud over his administration. He opposed the extension of slavery as well as the deposit of state funds in a national bank. His Jeffersonian ideas on limited government precluded policies that might have helped to alleviate the depression, and his popularity suffered accordingly. In 1840 he ran unsuccessfully for re-election as a Democrat and in 1848, as a member of the Free Soil Party.

William Henry Harrison

1773–1841
9TH PRESIDENT
Whig
Term: Mar 4–Apr 4, 1841
Vice-President:
John Tyler
First Lady:
Anna Symmes

William Henry Harrison's famous "log cabin" presidential campaign of 1840 created the impression that he was a frontier soldier in the mode of Andrew Jackson. On the contrary, Harrison was born in Charles City County, Virginia, the son of a wealthy planter. He studied medicine, then joined the army in 1791 and fought Native Americans in the Northwest Territory (now part of the Midwest). As territorial secretary, he went to Congress in 1798–9 and originated the first Homestead Law.

In 1800 Harrison became governor of Indiana Territory (to 1812) and led troops against Shawnee chief Tecumseh, who had rebelled against white incursions. Harrison's defeat of Tecumseh at the Battle of Tippecanoe (1811) made him a national figure, and his reputation grew during the War of 1812 with Great Britain. After the war he entered politics, serving in Congress until he ran for president in 1836 as the Whig candidate. Defeated that year, he was elected in 1840 on the slogan "Tippecanoe and Tyler too!" (John Tyler being his vice-presidential candidate). Unfortunately, Harrison contracted pneumonia during his inauguration and died only a month after moving into the White House.

John Tyler

1790–1862
10TH PRESIDENT
Whig
Term: Apr. 6, 1841–1845
Vice-President: None
First Ladies:
Letitia Christian (d. 1842)
Julia Gardiner (m. 1844)

Tyler was the first vice-president to succeed to the presidency upon the incumbent's death. A native of Charles City County, Virginia, he graduated from the College of William & Mary in 1807 and undertook the practice of law. In 1825 he was elected governor of Virginia (an office his father had held) and in 1827 became a U.S. Senator.

Tyler was elected vice-president on the Whig ticket with William Henry Harrison in 1840 in a colorful campaign that painted the two aristocratic Virginians as men of the people. A month after his inauguration, President Harrison died of pneumonia and Tyler took the oath of office. His Jeffersonian principles, including states' rights and opposition to a national bank, brought him into conflict with his own party, Congress, and his cabinet, all of whom, with the exception of Daniel Webster, resigned in 1841 at the instigation of Congressional leader Henry Clay. During Tyler's administration, the Republics of Texas and Florida were admitted to the Union.

Tyler retired from public life in 1845, but returned to Washington in 1861 to preside at the North-South peace conference that tried to prevent the Civil War. He was then elected to the Confederate Congress, but died before it convened.

James K. Polk

1795–1849
11TH PRESIDENT
Democrat
Term: 1845–49
Vice-President:
George M. Dallas
First Lady: Sarah Childress

Polk was president when the U.S. achieved its greatest territorial growth, largely as a result of the Mexican War of 1846–8. He was born in Mecklenberg County, North Carolina, to an emigrant family from Ireland and graduated from the University of North Carolina in 1818. Admitted to the Tennessee bar in 1820, he became prominent in local politics: his short stature and powerful rhetoric earned him the nickname "Napoleon of the Stump." He entered Congress in 1825 with the backing of Andrew Jackson.

In 1838 Polk was elected governor of Tennessee. An advocate of expansionism, he was nominated by the Democrats in 1844 as a dark horse candidate against the popular Henry Clay.

First lady Sarah Childress Polk was a devout Moravian, and card-playing, dancing, and drinking were banned from the White House during Polk's administration. He achieved his objectives, including settlement of the Oregon boundary dispute with Great Britain, reduction of the tariff, re-establishment of an independent treasury, and acquisition of California and Texas through the Mexican War, which also yielded territory that formed six other Western states. Nevertheless, Polk was the first president who did not actively seek re-election.

Zachary Taylor

1784–1850
12TH PRESIDENT
Whig
Term: Mar. 5, 1849–
Jul. 9, 1850
Vice-President: Millard Fillmore
First Lady: Margaret Smith

Zachary Taylor, a native of Orange County, Virginia, became president largely as a result of his successful military career, most notably his Mexican War victory over Santa Anna's superior force at the Battle of Buena Vista (1847). His nickname, "Old Rough and Ready," caught the public imagination, and President James K. Polk supported his nomination by the Whig Party in 1848.

Taylor's father had served in the Revolutionary War. Taylor himself was commissioned in 1808, and after serving in the War of 1812, he overcame the Sauk resistance to U.S. policies led by Chief Black Hawk.

In 1845 he was sent to Texas to defend against an expected invasion from Mexico, which had never relinquished its claim to the area. When the Mexican War broke out in 1846, Taylor and General Winfield Scott were the principal commanders of U.S. troops in the conflict.

As president, Taylor took a "no-compromise" attitude toward the growing rift between North and South, vowing to maintain the Union by force if necessary. However, he contracted cholera and died after sixteen months in office, to be succeeded by Vice-President Millard Fillmore.

Millard Fillmore

1800–74
13TH PRESIDENT
Whig
Term: Jul. 10, 1850–
Mar. 3, 1853
Vice-President: None
First Lady: Abigail Powers

The thirteenth president was the son of a frontier family from Locke, New York. Largely self-educated, Fillmore read law and opened his own practice in 1823. His talent for politics, and his advantageous marriage to socialite Abigail Powers, brought him to the New York State Assembly, where he became a leader of the Whig Party. In 1848 the Whigs chose him as Zachary Taylor's running mate.

Taylor had been opposed to the compromises proposed by Henry Clay to prevent the Union from splitting over the slavery issue. However, when Fillmore became president after Taylor's death in July 1850, he supported what became known as the Compromise of 1850. This legislation admitted California to the Union as a free state and created territorial governments for Utah and New Mexico. It abolished the slave trade in the District of Columbia and established the Fugitive Slave Law.

These stopgap measures prevented an outright breach in the Union, and Fillmore focused on economic improvements and made history with Commodore Perry's mission to Japan. He lost the Whig nomination in 1852 and was defeated in the 1856 election as a candidate for the Know-Nothing Party, after which he retired from politics.

Franklin Pierce

1804–69
14TH PRESIDENT
Democrat
Term: 1853–57
Vice-President:
William R. King
First Lady:
Jane Means Appleton

Elected at the age of forty-eight, Pierce was to be the youngest president until Theodore Roosevelt took office in 1901. The Democrats nominated him in 1852 because of his support for the Compromise of 1850, which sought to settle the slavery dispute.

Born in Hillsboro, New Hampshire, Pierce graduated from Bowdoin College in 1824, set up a law practice, and entered state politics while his father was governor of New Hampshire. In 1833 he was elected to Congress and the following year married Jane Means Appleton. Their marriage was fraught with difficulties, including Mrs. Pierce's long illness with tuberculosis and the depression from which she suffered after two of their three sons died in childhood. She disliked public life, and Pierce resigned from the Senate at her behest in 1842. He served as a brigadier general in the Mexican War under Winfield Scott and was nominated by the Democrats in 1852.

During Pierce's administration, the Gadsden Purchase (1853) added the huge Nebraska and Kansas Territories to the United States. However, Pierce's ill-advised support for the Kansas-Nebraska Act, which created a violent realignment of pro- and antislavery forces, lost him the Democratic nomination in 1856.

James Buchanan

1791–1868
15TH PRESIDENT
Democrat
Term: 1857–61
Vice-President:
John C. Breckinridge
First Lady: None (Bachelor)

James Buchanan needed all his skills as a diplomat to steer a course between rival factions of North and South during his term, but national tensions were erupting into civil war by the time he left office.

Buchanan was born near Mercersburg, Pennsylvania, and attended Dickinson College before practicing law. A lifelong bachelor, he had an early and distinguished career in Congress before serving as minister to Russia (1832–4). He was Polk's secretary of state during the Mexican War of 1846–8 and Franklin Pierce's minister to Great Britain and coauthor of the Ostend Manifesto (1854) on U.S. policies toward Cuba.

Buchanan became the Democrats' compromise candidate for the presidential election of 1856. He was personally opposed to slavery, but committed to states' rights, and Northern Democrats charged that he favored the South in the controversy over "Bleeding Kansas," where violence broke out between slavery and antislavery factions in 1856. The newly organized antislavery Republican Party nominated Congressman Abraham Lincoln for the critical election of 1860, and Buchanan left office in 1861 with an unblemished record of public service only to be made a scapegoat for the Civil War, after the fact.

Abraham Lincoln

1809–65
16TH PRESIDENT
Republican
Term: Mar. 4, 1861 -
Apr. 15, 1865

Vice Presidents:
Hannibal Hamlin, 1861–65
Andrew Johnson,
Mar. 4–Apr. 15, 1865
First Lady: Mary Todd

The man whom many regard as the nation's greatest president was born on a farm near Hodgenville, Kentucky, and moved with his family to Indiana at the age of seven. In 1830 they resettled near Decatur, Illinois. As a youth, Lincoln sailed with cargo boats to New Orleans and worked as a clerk in New Salem, Illinois. Largely self-educated, he read law and began his practice in Springfield, Illinois. In 1834 he was elected to the state legislature for the first of four terms. He married Mary Todd in 1842, and together they had four sons. Lincoln spent the 1847–9 term in the U.S. House of Representatives, but lost his backing when he criticized the Mexican War. In the mid-1850s he became the Illinois leader of the newly formed Republican Party, which he had left the Whigs to join.

In 1858 Lincoln ran as the Republican candidate for the U.S. Senate against Stephen A. Douglas, who was seeking re-election. Douglas won the election, but Lincoln attracted national attention during the famous Lincoln-Douglas debates on the issue of slavery, when he declared that "a house divided against itself cannot stand." In 1860 the Republicans nominated him for president under the slogan "The Union Must and Shall Be Preserved." The Southern states viewed his candidacy with alarm, and when he became the first Republican to be elected president, they began to secede from the Union. Seven had already done so by the time he was inaugurated on March 4, 1861. When Confederate guns opened fire on the federal installation at Fort Sumter in Charleston Harbor, South Carolina, Lincoln called for militia volunteers to put down the rebellion, and the nation's most severe crisis, the Civil War, was underway.

Throughout the war, Lincoln constantly faced harrowing decisions. Southern commanders including Robert E. Lee,

Thomas "Stonewall" Jackson, and Braxton Bragg repeatedly triumphed over such Northern generals as George McClellan and Benjamin Hooker for several years. Major draft riots broke out in New York City, and a protracted blockade against the Southern states almost caused armed conflict with Great Britain over trade rights.

On January 1, 1863, Lincoln's Emancipation Proclamation declared that all slaves in the rebellious states were thenceforth and forever free. Six months later the Union Army won the major Battle of Gettysburg, Pennsylvania, where Lincoln later delivered the single most famous speech in American history, the Gettysburg Address, honoring soldiers of both sides. Not until 1864, with the appointment of Ulysses S. Grant as commander-in-chief of Union forces, did Lincoln have the kind of generalship needed to end the war. Confederate general Robert E. Lee eventually surrendered on April 9, 1865, at Appomattox Court House, Virginia. By that time, Lincoln had won re-election, and he took office with the intention of reuniting the nation in the spirit of "kindness towards all, with malice towards none."

Tragically, he was shot less than six weeks later by actor John Wilkes Booth at Ford's Theatre in Washington and died the following morning, April 15, 1865. His funeral cortege, by train to Springfield, Illinois, witnessed an outpouring of grief that testified to the greatness of the man who had led the nation through its most harrowing trial.

Andrew Johnson

1808–75
17TH PRESIDENT
National Union
Term: Apr. 15, 1865–
Mar. 3, 1869
Vice-President: None
First Lady: Eliza McCardle

Thrust into the presidency by the assassination of Abraham Lincoln, Johnson, of rural Raleigh, North Carolina, faced tremendous adversities in early life. Apprenticed to a tailor at the age of ten, he did not learn to read and write until his marriage to Eliza McCardle in 1827. He became active in local politics and from 1843 represented the small farmers of eastern Tennessee in Congress (to 1856). Elected a senator in 1857, he was the only Southern senator to remain in office after his state seceded from the Union.

Johnson's record as a border-state Union supporter made him a desirable running mate for Lincoln in the 1864 campaign. After Lincoln's death, he sought to implement his predecessor's moderate plans for postwar reconstruction, but was balked by Congress. Radical Republicans overrode most of his vetoes and passed bills to restrict presidential authority. In defiance of the new Tenure of Office Act, Johnson dismissed Secretary of War Edwin M. Stanton in 1868, and impeachment proceedings were brought against him. Tried by the Senate on a variety of irrelevant charges, Johnson was acquitted by a single vote, but retired from office a bitter man. In 1875 he was elected to the Senate again, but he died a few months later.

Ulysses S. Grant

1822–85
18TH PRESIDENT
Republican
Term: 1869–77

Vice Presidents:
Schuyler Colfax, 1869–73
Henry Wilson, 1873–77
First Lady: Julia Boggs Dent

Civil War general and eighteenth president, Grant was born in Point Pleasant, Ohio, and attended the U.S. Military Academy at West Point, New York. He served in the Mexican War (1846–8) against his conscience, believing it to be unjust, and in 1848 he married Julia Dent. Heavy drinking led to his forced resignation from the army in 1854.

For some time Grant worked the property he called "Hardscrabble" in St. Louis, Missouri, and when the Civil War broke out he was clerking in the family store in Galena, Illinois. He became a colonel in an Illinois regiment and, after his first success, was made a general. His arduous campaigns in the western theater, notably the siege of Vicksburg (1863), impressed President Lincoln, who made him commander-in-chief of Union armies in 1864. He wore down Robert E. Lee's Confederate army until its surrender at Appomattox in April 1865.

Grant's military record made him a national hero, and he was elected president in 1868 and 1872. Unfortunately, he was a poor politician, and his second term was marred by government and financial scandals. His favoritism led him to appoint untrustworthy men to high office, and his support for the Radical Republicans, with their punitive policies toward the defeated South, kept alive the hatred engendered by the Civil War. Although he had taken office with the words "Let us have peace," his passivity and poor judgment made his presidency anticlimactic to his brilliant record as lieutenant general—the highest rank awarded to an American officer since Washington.

After leaving the White House, Grant lent his support to a New York banking house in which his son was involved. The firm went bankrupt in 1884. Suffering from cancer of the throat, and desperate with anxiety about the support of his family, he completed the manuscript for his monumental military history, *Personal Memoirs,* only days before his death.

Rutherford B. Hayes

1822–93
19TH PRESIDENT
Republican
Term: 1877–81
Vice-President:
William A. Wheeler
First Lady: Lucy Ware Webb

A native of Delaware, Ohio, Hayes attended Kenyon College and studied law at Harvard, graduating in 1845. He practiced in Cincinnati and married Lucy Webb in 1852. Hayes led a volunteer regiment from Ohio during the Civil War and was wounded four times. While still in service, he was elected to Congress (1864).

After the war, Hayes served as governor of Ohio for three terms and was nominated for the presidency by the Republicans in 1876. His opponent in the hotly contested election was Samuel Tilden, who had a narrow margin in the popular vote but needed one more electoral vote to win. Hayes was finally declared the winner by a special electoral commission. He promptly honored his campaign promise to withdraw Federal troops from the Southern states and end Reconstruction. He also restored public confidence in paper money by redeeming it with gold or silver.

Hayes's efforts to reform the civil service system were less successful, due mainly to opposition in Congress. In 1881 he retired into private life, focusing his attention on humanitarian and educational projects.

James A. Garfield

1831–81
20TH PRESIDENT
Republican
Term: Mar. 4–Sept. 19, 1881
Vice-President:
Chester A. Arthur
First Lady: Lucretia Rudolph

The twentieth president had been in office for only four months when he was shot by a disgruntled office seeker from his own Republican Party on July 2, 1881. He lingered until September 19 before succumbing to his wounds, retaining the powers of the presidency until his death.

Garfield was born into poverty in Orange, Ohio, but put himself through Hiram and Williams Colleges to become a teacher. Later, he returned to Hiram College as a professor and, eventually, as its president. After becoming a state senator, he married Lucretia Rudolph (1858). During the Civil War, he led a regiment of volunteers and became a major general. In 1863 he was elected a congressman from Ohio, a post in which he served for seventeen years.

Elected a U.S. senator in 1880, he was proposed as a dark-horse presidential candidate by the Republicans later that year. With Chester A. Arthur as his running mate, he was elected president. His assassination by lawyer Charles Giuteau, who had hoped to be appointed consul to France, highlighted the bitter divisions within the Republican Party and the need for civil service reform.

Chester A. Arthur

1829–86
21ST PRESIDENT
Republican
Term: Sept. 20, 1881–
Mar. 4, 1885
Vice-President: None
First Lady: None
(widowed 1880)

Chester Arthur's checkered career in New York State politics seemed to militate against his success as the president who unexpectedly succeeded James Garfield on September 20, 1881. However, he surprised his critics by taking a firm line on civil service reform and opposing political patronage to the detriment of his own prospects.

A native of Fairfield, Vermont, Arthur graduated from Union College in 1848, studied law, and established a successful practice in New York, where he became powerful in Republican politics. In 1871 he was made collector of the port of New York City, a federal post controlled by the state political machine. His reputation for dispensing patronage jobs led to his suspension by President Hayes in 1878. Undeterred, Arthur became head of New York City's party machine, and in 1880 the Stalwart faction of the Republican Party chose him as James A. Garfield's running mate.

As president, Arthur rose above partisanship to sign the Pendleton Civil Service Act, with its strict requirements for federal job candidates and a bipartisan Civil Service Commission to oversee its provisions. Arthur's confrontations with his own divided party cost him the presidential nomination in 1884.

Grover Cleveland

1837–1908
22ND & 24TH PRESIDENT
Democrat
Terms: 1885–89, 1893–97
Vice-Presidents:
Thomas A. Hendricks, 1885–89
Adlai E. Stevenson, 1893–97
First Lady: Frances Folsom

Stephen Grover Cleveland served two nonconsecutive terms as the first Democratic president since the Civil War. The son of a Presbyterian minister, he was born in Caldwell, New Jersey, and grew up in New York State. He studied law and was admitted to the bar in 1859.

Elected mayor of Buffalo in 1881, he reformed the city government and became governor of New York in 1882, despite the enmity of party bosses. In 1884 the Democrats nominated him for president on a reform platform. A vicious campaign was waged against him, but he was elected over James G. Blaine. He married Frances Folsom in the first White House wedding two years later. His push for lower tariffs cost him the backing of his party, and he lost the 1888 election to Benjamin Harrison in the electoral college, although he had a plurality of the popular vote.

Re-elected in 1892, Cleveland inherited the financial disorder left by the Harrison administration and was unfairly blamed for the Panic of 1893. During the Pullman railroad strike of 1894, he sent federal troops to guard the mails: the resulting violence led him to be branded antilabor. He was not renominated in 1896, and his accomplishments in reform and public service were scarcely recognized until after his death.

Benjamin Harrison

1833–1901
23RD PRESIDENT
Republican
Term: 1889–93
Vice-President: Levi P. Morton
First Lady:
Caroline Lavinia Scott

The grandson of President William Henry Harrison, and the son of a member of Congress, the twenty-third president was born in North Bend, Ohio, and graduated from Miami University (Oxford, Ohio) in 1852. His law practice in Indianapolis was interrupted by the Civil War, during which he commanded a regiment under William T. Sherman. After the war he returned to his practice and became active in Republican politics in Indiana.

Elected to the U.S. Senate in 1881, Harrison became nationally known: in 1889 the Republicans nominated him for president. He ran against Grover Cleveland, who had more popular votes, but Harrison won in the electoral college.

Harrison's pro-business views were an asset in a time of increasing prosperity. He supported high tariffs, but also initiated the Sherman Anti-Trust Act, which outlawed trusts and monopolies in restraint of trade. His national budget was of record size: nearly a billion dollars.

In the election of 1892, Harrison ran against Cleveland again, but this time Cleveland won. Widowed only two weeks before the election, Harrison returned to Indiana, where he resumed his law practice.

William McKinley

1843–1901
25TH PRESIDENT
Republican
Term: Mar. 4, 1897–Sept. 14, 1901
Vice-Presidents:
Garret A. Hobart, 1897–1899
Theodore Roosevelt,
Mar. 4, 1897–Sept. 14, 1901
First Lady: Ida Saxton

McKinley was born in Niles, Ohio, and attended Allegheny College. When the Civil War broke out in 1861, he joined the Ohio infantry as a private and rose to the rank of brevet major. He would become the last Civil War veteran to be elected president. After the war, he studied law, was admitted to the Ohio bar (1867), and supported the political career of his former commander, Rutherford B. Hayes.

McKinley was elected to Congress in 1876 and held office, except for one term, until 1891. He achieved prominence with the passage of the tariff bill of 1890 and became governor of Ohio for two years in 1891. He won the Republican presidential nomination in 1896 and won the election over populist William Jennings Bryan, who campaigned on a platform of free silver versus gold as the monetary standard. Bryan's famous "Cross of Gold" speech won him a place in the annals of American history, and McKinley had to espouse the gold standard as a result. In 1898 he tried to prevent the Spanish-American War, but popular opinion overruled him. On September 6, 1901, six months into his second term, he was shot by anarchist Leon Czolgosz at the Pan-American Exposition in Buffalo, New York. He died on September 14 and was succeeded by Theodore Roosevelt.

Theodore Roosevelt

1858–1919
26TH PRESIDENT
Republican
Terms: Sept. 14, 1901–
Mar. 3, 1909

Vice-Presidents:
None, 1901–05
Charles W. Fairbanks, 1905–09
First Lady:
Edith Kermit Carow

The twenty-sixth president overcame several severe health problems in childhood and the loss of his first wife, Alice Hathaway Lee, to carve out a distinguished political career. He addressed his health problems by a strenuous regime of outdoor activities that made him one of the first chief executives attuned to environmental concerns.

Born in New York City to an old and well-established family, he graduated from Harvard in 1880 and was soon elected to the New York State Assembly. After his marriage to Edith Kermit Carow in 1886, he served on the Civil Service Commission and presided over New York City's Board of Police Commissioners. In 1897 President McKinley appointed him assistant secretary of the navy. When the Spanish-American War was declared in 1898, Roosevelt led his own volunteer cavalry regiment, the "Rough Riders," in the famous charge on Cuba's San Juan (Kettle) Hill. In 1900, after serving as governor of New York, he ran for vice-president on McKinley's Republican ticket. After McKinley's assassination in September 1901, Roosevelt became the youngest man to serve as president.

During his first term, Roosevelt used aggressive policies to control trusts and break strikes. In his foreign relations, too, he followed his own advice to "carry a big stick." He promoted a revolution in Panama to create the interocean canal that united the Atlantic and Pacific fleets. His second term was known for his "Square Deal" policies, food and drug inspection laws, and mediation in the Russo-Japanese War (1905).

Roosevelt's hand-picked successor, William Howard Taft, won the election of 1908, but Roosevelt sought the Republican nomination again in 1912. When he failed to get it, he ran as the candidate for his own Progressive or "Bull Moose" Party. This split in the Republican Party was instrumental in bringing election victory to Democrat Woodrow Wilson.

William Howard Taft

1857–1930
27TH PRESIDENT
Republican
Term: 1909–13
Vice-President:
James S. Sherman
First Lady: Helen Herron

A native of Cincinnati, Ohio, Taft was a jurist rather than a politician. He studied law after graduating from Yale University in 1878 and became a judge of the Ohio superior court (1887–90)—the third generation of his family to serve as a judge. He married Helen Herron in 1886, and they had a daughter and two sons, both of whom entered politics.

Appointed solicitor general by President Benjamin Harrison in 1890, he became a federal circuit judge in 1892. Eight years later, he was made head of the Philippine Commission and governed the islands from 1901 to 1904. As President Theodore Roosevelt's secretary of war (from 1904), he became a trusted advisor and was Roosevelt's choice as his successor.

Progressive Republican support diminished after Taft's election, with his signature of the high-tariff Payne-Aldrich Act of 1909. His administration saw Arizona and New Mexico admitted as states, the continuation of "trust busting," and strengthened control of the railroads. "Big Bill" Taft, as he was called for his 332-pound girth, lost the election of 1912 because of the Republican Party split. In 1921 he attained the highest judicial office and became the first man to have served as both president and chief justice of the Supreme Court.

Woodrow Wilson

1856–1924
28TH PRESIDENT
Democrat
Terms: 1913–21
Vice-President: Thomas R. Marshall
First Ladies:
Ellen Louise Axson (d. 1914)
Edith Bolling Galt (m. 1915)

Statesman and educator Woodrow Wilson is often associated with New Jersey's Princeton University, where he studied, taught, and served as president (1902–10). However, he was a Southerner, born in Staunton, Virginia.

Elected governor of New Jersey in 1910, his liberal reforms impressed his party, which nominated him for president in 1912. He defeated President Taft and Progressive Theodore Roosevelt to become the first Democratic president in fifteen years.

His legislation included the Federal Reserve Act of 1913, the Clayton Antitrust Act of 1914, and the Child Labor Act of 1915. He was re-elected in 1916 on the slogan "He kept us out of war," but German submarine attacks on American shipping led him to ask Congress to declare war on Germany five months after his second inauguration on grounds that "the world must be made safe for democracy." He attended the Paris peace conference in 1919 and persuaded the European powers to adopt his Fourteen Points, including establishment of a peace-keeping League of Nations. However, the U.S. Senate refused to ratify membership in it. Wilson suffered a severe stroke in October 1919; he served out his term as an invalid and died only five years later.

Warren G. Harding

1865–1923
29TH PRESIDENT
Republican
Term: Mar. 4, 1921–Aug. 2, 1923
Vice-President: Calvin Coolidge
First Lady:
Florence Kling DeWolfe

The twenty-ninth president was a journalist before he entered politics and proved extremely popular with the press until the scandals that undermined his health and reputation emerged midway through his term. Born on a farm in Corsica, Ohio, Harding attended Ohio Central College and bought the Marion *Star,* a small Ohio newspaper, in 1884. His marriage to the ambitious widow Florence Kling DeWolfe helped the paper to prosper, and Harding held several state offices before his election to the U.S. Senate in 1914. In 1920 the Republicans chose him as their candidate for president because of his party loyalty.

Advocating a "return to normalcy" and rejection of President Wilson's postwar policies, Harding chose his advisors unwisely from political cronies known as "The Ohio Gang." An honest man himself, he was deeply dismayed by the spree of bribery and corruption that culminated in the infamous Teapot Dome and Veterans' Bureau scandals. The worst offenders were Secretary of the Treasury Andrew Mellon, Attorney General Harry Daugherty, and Secretary of the Interior Albert B. Fall. In 1923, shortly after the scandals were revealed, Harding developed pneumonia and died, leaving the presidency to Calvin Coolidge.

Calvin Coolidge

1872–1933
30TH PRESIDENT
Republican
Term: Aug. 3, 1923–Mar. 3, 1929
Vice-President:
None, 1923–25
Charles G. Dawes, 1925–9
First Lady:
Grace Anna Goodhue

John Calvin Coolidge was born on a farm near Plymouth, Vermont, and graduated from Amherst College in 1895. He studied law and began a practice in Northampton, Massachusetts. In 1905 he married Grace Anna Goodhue. He rose from local and state offices to governor of Massachusetts in 1919 and was nominated to run as Warren G. Harding's vice-president at the Republican convention of 1920.

Harding died of pneumonia on August 2, 1923, and Coolidge, visiting in Vermont, was sworn in as president by his own father, a notary public. In office, he advocated economy in government and minimal regulation of business. This proved an unfortunate policy, as the unrestrained speculation of the "Roaring Twenties" would precipitate the Great Depression in 1929.

Coolidge was re-elected in 1924, with Charles G. Dawes as vice-president. "Keep cool with Coolidge" was the slogan of the day. Prosperity increased and foreign affairs presented no pressing problems. In mid-1927, the laconic Coolidge announced: "I do not choose to run for President in 1928." He returned to Northampton after leaving office, resumed the practice of law, and occasionally contributed articles on current affairs to newspapers and magazines.

Herbert Hoover

1874–1964
31ST PRESIDENT
Republican
Term: 1929–33
Vice-President: Charles Curtis
First Lady: Lou Henry

A mining engineer and multimillionaire whose dynamic career took him around the world, Herbert Hoover graduated from Stanford University in 1895 and married Lou Henry, whom he had met in his senior year, in 1899.

During World War I he gained national renown as the "great humanitarian" through his relief work for European civilians in the war zone. From 1921 until 1928, he served creditably as secretary of commerce under both Warren G. Harding and Calvin Coolidge. His solid reputation assured him the Republican presidential nomination and the election.

When Hoover took office in 1929, the economy was booming, but just a short time later came the disastrous economic crash that ushered in the great Depression, leaving 12 million people unemployed and bringing poverty to many more. Convinced that the federal government should not intervene in the realm of economics—believing that the depression would resolve itself—he did not institute any federal welfare programs, but assured the public in good faith that "Prosperity is just around the corner." The fact that it wasn't led to Franklin D. Roosevelt's overwhelming victory in the 1932 election.

Franklin D. Roosevelt

1882–1945
32ND PRESIDENT
Democrat
Term: Mar. 4, 1933–
Apr. 12, 1945
Vice-Presidents:
John N. Garner, 1933–41
Henry A. Wallace, 1941–45
Harry S. Truman,
Jan. 30–Apr. 12, 1945
First Lady: Anna Eleanor Roosevelt

The only man to be elected president four times, Franklin D. Roosevelt was a fifth cousin of Theodore Roosevelt, whose niece, Eleanor Roosevelt, married FDR in 1905. Born in Hyde Park, New York, he graduated from Harvard in 1904 and began practicing law in New York City. In 1910 he was elected to the New York Senate and in 1913 became assistant secretary of the navy. Handsome, charismatic, and confident, his political future seemed assured.

In 1921 FDR suffered an attack of polio that left his legs paralyzed, but he recovered his strength sufficiently to stand with crutches and braces. His physical disability was concealed from the public. In 1928 he was elected governor of New York State, and in 1932 he ran successfully for the presidency against Herbert Hoover, taking office in the midst of the Great Depression.

On the eve of his inauguration, FDR was faced with the immediate crisis of the collapse of the nation's banking system, a calamity that resulted from a nationwide panic. The onslaught of millions of citizens demanding that their savings be returned to them was more than the nation's banks could handle. FDR assured the people that he would rectify this crisis in a speech that is now famous for its moving declaration that "the only thing we have to fear is fear itself." Within a week emergency banking legislation was passed and the banks received the liquidity that they needed to rectify the situation. Confidence in their new president was demonstrated by the nation when millions returned to the banks to redeposit their savings.

FDR launched a series of policies designed to afford national relief from the economic crisis, which had seen 5,000 bank failures and left millions unemployed. He introduced the New Deal, appropriating $7 billion to restore buying power and reemploy as many people as possible through government agencies.

The New Deal was an innovative program that was responsible for enacting domestic legislation on a nationwide scale. Maximum working hours were set and a minimum wage was created. Those who were out of work found assistance in the introduction of unemployment insurance, and retired Americans were guaranteed an income with the new social security program.

FDR's second term as president was marked by the commencement of World War II in September 1939. Although he made it clear that his sympathies lay with the Allied Powers, FDR decided to avoid bringing America into the war for as long as possible. He knew that the terrible memory of the first World War was still vivid in the minds of many Americans. However, FDR continued to champion the cause of the Allies by assisting them in purchasing American weaponry. FDR explained these measures to the public via radio broadcasts that were called "fireside chats," winning enormous public confidence.

In 1936 FDR was re-elected by the greatest plurality any candidate had ever received and continued to implement his domestic programs. In January 1941, he made his famous "Four Freedoms" announcement, declaring that "all people are entitled to freedom of speech and worship and freedom from want and fear." The catalyst behind this statement was FDR's increasing disgust with the actions and words of Adolf Hitler. In August 1941, FDR met with Prime Minister Winston Churchill on a war vessel that was stationed off the coast of Newfoundland. Together they created the Atlantic Charter, which was based on the desire to end tyranny and established plans for a new world order. Fifteen countries, including the USSR, endorsed the charter.

In 1940 FDR became the first president to be elected to a third term. On December 7 of that same year, Japanese war planes bombed Pearl Harbor, Hawaii. Under FDR the United States took decisive action and declared war on Japan the day after the bombing. Three days later, on December 11, the United States became an integral force in World War II when Germany and Italy declared war on the nation. At the Arcadia Conference, which was held in Washington from December 22, 1941, to January 14, 1942, FDR and Churchill agreed that their involvement in the war would not cease until the Axis Powers had been defeated. FDR remained true to his word and continued to be a vigorous war leader whose last appearance as a dominant member of the Allied "Big Three"—himself, Winston Churchill, and Josef Stalin—was at the Yalta Conference of February 1945. FDR died suddenly two months later, his health worn down by the strain of the war, leaving the presidency and the conclusion of World War II to Harry S. Truman.

Harry S. Truman

1884–1972
33RD PRESIDENT
Democrat
Term: Apr. 12, 1945–
Jan. 20, 1953
Vice-President:
Alben W. Barkley, 1949–53
First Lady: Elizabeth (Bess)
Virginia Wallace

A native of Lamar, Missouri, Harry Truman hoped to attend the U.S. Military Academy at West Point, but was refused on account of his poor eyesight. Nevertheless, he was a distinguished captain of field artillery in World War I. In 1919 he married Bess Wallace after a long courtship and opened a men's store in Kansas City, Missouri. When it failed during the recession of 1921–2, he spent nearly fifteen years paying off his debts rather than declare personal bankruptcy.

While serving as a county judge, Truman studied law in Kansas City and worked to gain the support of the powerful Kansas City Democratic political machine. He served as presiding county judge (1926–34) and was first elected to the U.S. Senate in 1934. Re-elected in 1940, he earned national renown for his determination and integrity as chairman of the Committee to Investigate the National Defense during World War II, saving the country some $15 billion in expenditures. During the presidential campaign of 1944, Truman was nominated as Franklin D. Roosevelt's vice-president on the second ballot, and they were elected easily. Upon Roosevelt's sudden death on April 12, 1945, shortly before the end of World War II, Truman became president.

Major decisions faced Truman from his first hour in office and throughout his presidency. He approved use of the atomic bomb on Hiroshima and Nagasaki in August 1945 on military advice that it would end the war in the Pacific, a controversial decision that reverberates to the present day. At Potsdam, he met with Prime Minister Winston Churchill and Premier Josef Stalin, becoming the newest member of the "Big Three" world leaders. After the war, he sponsored the Marshall Plan, which offered massive financial assistance to European countries devastated by the conflict. In 1947 he abandoned America's long-held isolationist stance when he announced the "Truman Doctrine," whereby the United States would assist noncommunist countries against communist encroachment. Its effects throughout the Cold War decades were incalculable.

Where FDR had used the radio for his famous "fireside chats" to increase his popularity and profile, Truman made the first television broadcast from the White House in 1947, an event that finally brought the president into full public view. Truman's most memorable television appearance occurred in 1952, when he led a tour through the White House. The influence of the media was thenceforth to transform presidential politics.

Truman was famous for the phrase "The buck stops here," and after his surprise re-election over Thomas E. Dewey in 1948, he had reason to prove it again when the Korean War broke out in 1950. He committed U.S. troops to the defense of noncommunist South Korea when it was invaded by communist North Korea and recalled General Douglas MacArthur, who wanted to extend the war into communist China. After a demanding life in public service, he retired in 1953 without seeking a second full term as president.

Dwight D. Eisenhower

1890–1969

34TH PRESIDENT

Republican

Term: 1953–61

Vice-President:
Richard M. Nixon

First Lady:
Mary (Mamie) Geneva Doud

The thirty-fourth president was a distinguished military man who served as Allied commander-in-chief during World War II. Born in Denison, Texas, Dwight D. Eisenhower grew up in Abilene, Kansas, and attended the U.S. Military Academy at West Point. In 1916, a year after he graduated, he married Mamie Doud.

Eisenhower's steady rise through staff and command assignments resulted in his being put in charge of war plans after the United States entered World War II in 1941. The following year he became commander of U.S. troops in Europe and directed the invasions of North Africa and Italy. In 1943 he was made supreme Allied commander in Europe, where as such he executed the invasion of France through the Normandy coast (June 1944) and directed the Allied drive on Berlin. The defeat of Hitler resulted in Eisenhower's image as an American war hero, even though he had never fought in a battle.

After the war Eisenhower was named U.S. army chief of staff, a post in which his brilliant talent as a military administrator was put to good use. He also served as president of New York City's Columbia University between 1948 and 1950, publishing his memoir *Crusade in Europe* in 1948. In 1952 he was urged to run for president by both the Democratic and Republican parties. He retired from the army and won the Republican nomination on the first ballot, defeating the popular Adlai E. Stevenson in the election and becoming the first Republican president since Herbert Hoover.

Eisenhower's standing was confirmed when he visited U.S. military units in South Korea and supported the social and economic programs of previous Democratic administrations. He adhered to the Truman Doctrine in opposing the spread of communism into new areas and sponsored ambitious public works programs, including the interstate highway system. He was re-elected in 1956 despite the fact that he had suffered a heart attack the previous year. "I like Ike," the campaign slogan based on his nickname, prevailed at the polls again. As before, he visited heads of state around the world, contributing to the creation of an international postwar community that did not include the USSR, with whom Cold-War tensions were escalating. In 1961 Eisenhower terminated diplomatic relations with Fidel Castro's increasingly militant Cuban government and began a determined, though unsuccessful, campaign to oust Castro.

Among Eisenhower's greatest domestic challenges was the desegregation of schools across the South: he stated that "there must be no second-class citizens in this country." In 1959 the states of Hawaii and Alaska were admitted to the Union, bringing the total number of stars on the American flag to fifty.

Eisenhower was seventy when he retired in 1961 to his farm in Gettysburg, Pennsylvania. After his retirement from public life, he published his political memoirs in three volumes: *The White House Years* (1963–5).

John F. Kennedy

1917–63
35TH PRESIDENT
Democrat
Term: Jan. 20, 1961–
Nov. 22, 1963

Vice-President:
Lyndon B. Johnson
First Lady: Jacqueline (Jackie)
Lee Bouvier

At forty-three, John Fitzgerald Kennedy became the first Roman Catholic to be elected president. He came from a family of Irish descent, long powerful in Boston and Massachusetts politics. The second of nine children born in Brookline, Massachusetts, he was educated at Harvard and commanded a PT (patrol torpedo) boat in the Pacific during World War II, rescuing his crew after the craft was sunk. Decorated for heroism, he entered politics in 1946, served three terms in the House, and became U.S. senator from Massachusetts in 1952. The following year, he married Jacqueline Lee Bouvier, who became a distinct asset to his political career. They had three children, of whom two, John and Caroline, lived to maturity.

In 1960 Kennedy was nominated for president by the Democrats with Texan Lyndon Baines Johnson as his running mate. His election victory owed much to his television debates with Richard Nixon, in which he impressed the public with his cool maturity as well as his handsome, articulate presence.

Kennedy faced several major problems during his term, beginning with the bungled Bay of Pigs invasion of communist-dominated Cuba (April 1961). Kennedy met with Soviet premier Nikita Khrushchev in Vienna that summer and faced him down the following year in the Cuban Missile Crisis. In 1963 he concluded treaty arrangements with the Soviets to limit the testing of nuclear weapons. At home, he took a firm stand on desegregation across the South, negotiating with state and city officials to minimize violent civil unrest. The high public hopes for his administration were cut short on November 22, 1963, when he was assassinated in Dallas during a speaking tour. Vice-President Johnson was immediately sworn in as president. The Warren Commission's investigation finally ruled that Kennedy's sole assassin was Lee Harvey Oswald, but theories of conspiracy have persisted in some quarters to the present day.

Lyndon Baines Johnson

1908–73
36TH PRESIDENT
Democrat
Term: Nov. 22, 1963–Jan. 20, 1969
Vice-President:
Hubert H. Humphrey
First Lady: Claudia ("Lady Bird")
Alta Taylor

Born on his family's farm near Stonewall, Texas, Lyndon Baines Johnson attended Southwest Texas State Teachers College and taught history in Houston before going to Washington, D.C., as a Congressional secretary. In 1934, after a two-month courtship, he married Claudia Alta Taylor, known by her nickname of Lady Bird. In 1935 he began a two-year stint as administrator for a public works program in Texas, and in 1937 he was elected to the House of Representatives.

During World War II, Johnson served as a lieutenant commander in the U.S. Navy, after which he was elected to the Senate (1948) where he served until 1961. He had an unerring instinct for politics and rose rapidly to the position of Democratic majority leader (1955–61). With the cooperation of Sam Rayburn, Speaker of the House, he was instrumental in passing major legislation, including the first major Civil Rights bill since 1875. He made a bid for the Democratic presidential nomination in 1960, but was nominated instead as John F. Kennedy's running mate, balancing the ticket between the Northeast and the Southwest. As Kennedy's vice-president, Johnson served as the president of the Senate until the time of Kennedy's assassination on November 22, 1963. After the assassination, Johnson assumed the presidency.

Once in office, Johnson declared a national war on poverty and his domestic program, called "the Great Society," was directed toward increasing prosperity while reducing racism and unemployment. This program gained widespread political and public support as a result of the burgeoning Civil Rights movement. After his victory in the election of 1964, Congress responded to Johnson's triumph by passing legislation that continued his domestic program. In 1964 and 1965, Congress approved federal aid to elementary and secondary education, passed the Medicare program, and created the Department of Housing and Urban Development. Johnson's presidency also saw the passage of the Voting Rights Act of 1965, which was instrumental in registering a quarter of a million new black voters.

However, the increasingly unpopular U.S. involvement in the Vietnam War began to erode Johnson's popularity after his re-election in 1964. Secretary of Defense Robert S. McNamara and his colleagues in the Pentagon pushed hard for escalation of the conflict while concealing all they could from the public, but when the devastating images of the war carried by newspapers and television became widespread, there was a groundswell of outrage. Students, minority leaders, and affluent members of the middle class made common cause in protesting the war and leaving the country to avoid the draft. The outbreak of urban race riots in 1965 and 1968 served to further deplete Johnson's popularity, and in 1968 Johnson showed his political acumen by refusing to run for re-election. He retired to his LBJ ranch near Johnson City, Texas, and died in 1973—a day before the Vietnam war finally ended.

Richard M. Nixon

1913–94
37TH PRESIDENT
Republican
Term: Jan. 20, 1969–
Aug. 9, 1974

Vice-Presidents:
Spiro T. Agnew, 1969–
Oct. 10, 1973 (resigned)
Gerald R. Ford,
Oct. 11, 1973–Aug. 9, 1974
First Lady: Thelma (Pat) Ryan

The first president to resign from office, Nixon was a native of Yorba Linda, California. He graduated from Whittier College in 1934 and received his law degree from Duke University in 1937. An aggressive politician, he won election to the House of Representatives in 1946. He was an active member of the House Un-American Activities Committee and sponsored a bill to control communism in the United States (1948). He then served in the Senate from 1950 until 1952, when he was nominated as Dwight D. Eisenhower's running mate.

Nixon was Eisenhower's vice-president during both his terms. In 1960 he went on to seek the Republican presidential nomination, which he won, but he lost the election to John F. Kennedy. In 1962 he was disappointed in hopes of the California governorship and retired from politics until 1968, when he defeated Hubert Humphrey for the presidency with strong backing from business interests.

During Nixon's first term, he established détente with China and the USSR—a foreign relations coup that increased his popularity. However, he continued the unpopular war in Southeast Asia until late in his first term, when Henry Kissinger advised him to begin withdrawal of American troops. Nixon also pursued strong measures to fight inflation.

Re-elected by a wide margin in 1972 over George McGovern, Nixon ended American involvement in the Vietnam War. However, a break-in at Democratic headquarters in the Watergate complex sparked off an investigation into Nixon's re-election campaign practices that burgeoned into a highly publicized scandal involving top White House aides. The question of Nixon's own knowledge of Watergate led to impeachment hearings, and in July 1974 a House committee approved three articles of impeachment against him. On August 8, 1974, Nixon announced his resignation.

Ronald W. Reagan

b. 1911
40TH PRESIDENT
Republican
Term: 1981–89
Vice-President:
George H.W. Bush
First Lady: Anne (Nancy)
Frances Robbins Davis

A native of Tampico, Illinois, Ronald Reagan had an unusual second career in politics that followed thirty-two years in the entertainment business as a radio broadcaster and successful film actor. He was president of the Screen Actors Guild and represented the General Electric Company in a public relations capacity before entering politics in 1966.

Originally a Democrat, Reagan became a Republican in 1962 and worked for conservative causes. He was elected governor of California in 1966 and re-elected in 1970. He advocated cutting the cost of government, especially for welfare and education.

Defeated for the Republican nomination for the presidency in 1976 by President Gerald Ford, Reagan won by an overwhelming margin in 1980. In the election, he prevailed over Jimmy Carter by a wide margin in the electoral college. Once in office, Reagan proposed spending and income tax cuts for three successive years. On March 31, 1981, he was badly wounded by an assassin, but he made a rapid recovery, and his popularity remained high. His faith in "supply-side economics" proved ill placed, as his two administrations saw the largest budget deficits on record. He defeated Walter Mondale in the 1984 election and survived the Iran-Contra scandal of 1986 to retire from public life in 1989.

George H. W. Bush

b. 1924
41ST PRESIDENT
Republican
Term: 1989–93
Vice-President:
J. Danforth (Dan) Quayle
First Lady:
Barbara Pierce

George Bush was born in Milton, Massachusetts, and grew up in Connecticut and Maine. He graduated from Phillips Academy in 1942 and piloted a torpedo bomber in the U.S. Navy in World War II—the youngest man to do so.

After the war, Bush married Barbara Pierce, graduated from Yale University, and settled in Texas, where he cofounded Zapata Petroleum. He was elected to the House of Representatives in 1966. He served two terms and was appointed Permanent Representative to the United Nations in 1971. He was chairman of the Republican National Committee during the Watergate scandal, represented the United States in China, and served as director of the Central Intelligence Agency (1976). Bush sought the Republican presidential nomination in 1980, but instead was elected Ronald Reagan's vice-president (1981–9).

In 1988 Bush was elected president, and his experience with foreign affairs proved extremely valuable when the breakup of the Soviet Union began (1989). In 1990–91 he organized an international coalition to defeat the Iraqi dictator Saddam Hussein. It was his domestic policy that cost Bush a second term, as he was held to account for the business recession of 1992 and defeated in that year's election by William J. (Bill) Clinton.

William J. Clinton

b. 1946
42ND PRESIDENT
Democrat
Term: 1993–Present

Vice-President:
Albert Gore, Jr.
First Lady:
Hillary Diane Rodham

A native of Hope, Arkansas, the 42nd president was born William Jefferson Blythe IV, three months after his father died in an automobile accident. He was later adopted by his stepfather, Roger Clinton. He attended Georgetown University in Washington, D.C., and studied in England at Oxford University as a Rhodes Scholar during the Vietnam War. He met fellow law student Hillary Rodham at Yale University's School of Law, and they married in 1975.

Clinton served as attorney-general of Arkansas from 1977 until 1978, when he was elected governor of Arkansas at the age of thirty-two. Two years later, he lost his bid for re-election, but he regained the governor's seat in 1982 and held it through three subsequent elections. He was perceived as a populist progressive who worked to improve public education and diversify his state's economy.

In 1992 he won the three-way presidential election against Republican George Bush and independent candidate Ross Perot. Clinton's promises of sweeping reforms in health care foundered during his first year in office, but he succeeded in introducing other progressive social policies. After the mid-term election of 1994, a large new Republican majority in the House placed the issues of deficit reduction and a balanced budget at center stage. Internationally, Clinton faced conflict in the Balkans, Somalia, and Haiti, as well as the difficult transition to democracy in the former Soviet bloc. His objectives included the promotion of peace in Northern Ireland and the Middle East.

Clinton was renominated by the Democrats in 1996 and won the election over Republican Robert Dole and independent candidate Ross Perot by aiming at the center on such issues as fiscal policy, crime reduction, and party politics. Focusing on deficit reduction, he explored new approaches to balancing the budget, including Medicare, Medicaid, education, and the environment.